Wisdom for Living Spiritually with Money

How Important is Money?

Dr. Tommy S. W. Wong

Copyright © 2022 by Tommy S. W. Wong
All rights reserved
First edition

Printed in the United States of America

Dedicated to

my parents, Wong Sze Fong and Woo En Yueh

my parents-in-law, Sum Chip Shing and Ko Luk Ying

my darling wife, Christina

and my wonderful sons, Alston, Lester and Hanson

Acknowledgement

I like to thank the Great Spirit for selecting me as an instrument in authoring this book for the benefit of mankind.

Preface

Money is an essential part of life when we live physically on Earth. So, how can we live spiritually with money? In this sixth book in the "*Spiritual Living*" series, a young man, Tom, discusses this soul searching question with Guru Harry, who is a spirit and practices spirituality that is not religious. In their discussion, they explore the following deep questions:

(1) How does money relate to the physical needs of a body?
(2) How important is money to the poor and to the rich?
(3) How come the spiritual masters can say "no" to money so easily?
(4) How can we give kindness for free?
(5) What are the characteristics of money as compared with those of morality?

May this wisdom enable you to live spiritually with money in a physical, practical society!

Tommy S. W. Wong
Singapore
February 2022

Table of Contents

Chapter 1	Conversation with Guru Harry (Part 1)	1
Chapter 2	Conversation with Guru Harry (Part 2)	17
Chapter 3	Conversation with Guru Harry (Part 3)	35
Chapter 4	Conversation with Guru Harry (Part 4)	59
Chapter 5	Conversation with Guru Harry (Part 5)	75
Chapter 6	Conversation with Guru Harry (Part 6)	93
Appendix A	Letter from grandfather to grandson	101

Chapter 1

Conversation with Guru Harry (Part 1)

Hello Guru Harry, I'm here again.

Hello Tom, it's good to see you here again.

You know it's been some time since I last came, how have you been?

You know for the spiritual, we are always fine.

And your spirituality is non-religious, right?

Nope, I'm spiritual but not religious.

Have you ever been rich, Guru Harry?

Yeah sure, you mean spiritually rich?

No, I mean have you been financially rich?

You mean dollars and cents?

Yes, have you ever had a lot of money?

You know for us souls living in Heaven, we don't need money to live.

Because souls need nothing?

That's right, Tom. We don't need anything and we live forever.

But how about when you were living on Earth with a physical body?

Ah, that's different. Living on Earth with a physical body is a completely different ball game.

How different?

When I was on Earth with a physical body, I needed money alright.

Then, have you ever had a lot of money when you were on Earth?

Well, let's say I always had enough money to do whatever I wanted.

That's pretty good, right?

Yeah, I would say so.

Then, you must have had a lot of money.

Actually, I didn't.

Oh?

Because I didn't need a lot of money to do what I wanted.

Hmm, then how did you live?

I lived simply.

You mean you didn't buy expensive items?

Nope, and I didn't have expensive hobbies.

So, you lived a really simple life?

Yep, and that's a pretty good way to live, I say.

How about the luxuries in life?

What about the luxuries in life?

Wouldn't it be nice to live a life of luxury?

But that could be quite meaningless.

Wouldn't you like to have a big car and live in a big house?

That could be quite meaningless too.

How about traveling the world in style?

That too could be meaningless.

Why are these activities meaningless?

Because if I enjoy these luxuries, they are only good for me.

Then, how would you like to live?

I prefer to live meaningfully.

You mean you prefer to live a meaningful life?

Yes, a life with meaning.

But how?

By doing meaningful things.

What are the meaningful things you like to do?

Do good to others and create a better world.

Oh, but you mean doing these meaningful things don't cost money?

Some of these meaningful things can be accomplished with little or no money.

Wow, this sounds intriguing, Guru Harry.

Yes, it is, isn't it?

Okay, this is why I've come to see you this time.

Oh yes, why have you come, Tom?

I have come to discuss with you a very practical subject when we are living physically on Earth.

Okay, what is the practical subject?

Money.

Whoa, it is indeed a very practical subject.

And more specifically, how important is money when we live on Earth?

This is a really important question.

And practical, right?

Yes, it is a really important and practical question.

So, do we need money when we live physically on Earth?

Sure, money makes the world go round.

Woohoo, and this comes from Guru Harry.

Why? You sound surprised?

Because money is the root of all evil, right?

Is it?

That's what they say.

Yes, they do, don't they?

So, money can't be spiritual, right?

Hmm, actually, everything can be spiritual, Tom.

You mean everything including money can be spiritual?

Yep, it just depends on how we see that thing.

You mean it depends on how we see money?

Yes, actually it depends on how we use money.

Can you elaborate?

You see money is neutral. We can use it to do good or to do evil.

So, money may not be the root of all evil after all?

Nope, it depends on how it is used.

So, money can be spiritual?

If you use it to do good.

What kind of goodness is considered spiritual?

Doing good to others.

You mean help ever, hurt never?

That's pretty good.

And spiritual too?

Yes, it is in fact the essence of spirituality.

You mean do good to others?

Yes Tom, if you use money to do good to others, it is spiritual.

So, money can be part of a spiritual life?

Sure, we can use money spiritually.

But how does money fit into a physical life?

You have asked a very physical question.

Yes, how does money fit into a physical, practical life?

You have asked a very physical, practical question.

Yes, Guru Harry, can you share with me your spiritual perspective on how money fits into a physical, practical life?

Well, before I do that, how about I share with you a physical perspective on how money fits into a physical, practical life first?

Okay, whatever you think is best for me to have a good understanding on money.

Let's start by reviewing the needs of a physical body, shall we?

Sure, let's start.

Have you heard of Maslow's hierarchy of needs?

Yes, according to Maslow, there are five levels of needs.

What are the first level needs?

They are the physiological needs.

Yes, they are the basic needs of a body.

And they are air, water, food, clothing and shelter.

Correct, and the body cannot function without them.

So, the body really needs them just to keep itself going.

Do you need money to satisfy these needs?

Well, air is generally free, but sometimes, we may even have to pay for clean air. As for the other needs, we usually have to pay for them.

That's right. Do you know what is this payment generally referred as?

You mean the "cost of living"?

Very good Tom, this is the cost one has to pay just to get the basic needs of a body.

And this cost can be very high in some societies, right?

Yes, too high.

Is this why in these societies, many are obsessed with making a living?

Yep, because they need to get their heads above water.

You mean they need to get their basic needs?

Yes, otherwise, they cannot live.

You mean they'll die?

This is also why the poor really have to struggle just to be alive in these societies.

So, it is good to keep the cost of living low?

Yes, if the cost of living is low, the poor can have a reasonable standard of living.

You mean a humane standard of living?

Yes, so that the poor can live humanely.

And a good government will keep this cost low, right?

Haha Tom, you are now going into politics.

Well, the cost of living is intricately linked to the government policies, right?

Yes, very much so. This is why we need good people in governments to set good policies.

So that the poor can have a reasonable standard of living.

Yes Tom, what are the second level needs?

They are the safety needs.

What are the safety needs?

Protection, security, order, law, stability, and freedom from fear.

Do you need money to satisfy these needs?

Sure, and some needs can cost a lot of money.

Yes, especially protection from other humans.

You mean humans are our own worst enemy?

Just look at the defense budgets.

You mean we are defending from other humans?

And yet, we are all humans.

So, humans can actually save a lot of money if we can live at peace with each other.

Yes, like "we are all one".

You mean we can save a lot of money if we live as one humanity?

Yes Tom, what are the third level needs?

They are the love and belonging needs.

You mean friendship, intimacy, trust and acceptance, receiving and giving affection and love?

Yes, and to be part of groups like family, friends, and workmates.

Do you need money to satisfy these needs?

Some people pay a lot of money to try to have these needs satisfied.
You mean like love?

Yes, especially love.

But do they get real love?

Probably not, but they still willingly pay for it.

Why?

Maybe they are desperate.

Yes Tom, people are desperate for love.

So, they willingly pay even though the love is not real?

Yes Tom, what are the fourth level needs?

They are the esteem needs.

What are the esteem needs?

Achievement, status, recognition, fame, prestige, attention, strength, competence, mastery, self-confidence, independence, freedom, self-respect, and respect from others.

Do you need money to get these needs?

You may need money, a lot of money to satisfy some of these needs, but some of these needs can be satisfied for free.

Interesting!

Yes, in a good cultured society, independence, freedom, self-respect, and respect from others are free.

So, to satisfy some of these higher level needs, they may cost less than the lower level needs.

But some may cost more.

Yes Tom, what are the fifth level needs?

They are the self-actualization needs.

What are the self-actualization needs?

They are realizing personal potential, self-fulfillment, seeking personal growth and peak experiences.

Do you need money to satisfy these needs?

Hmm, I'm not too sure about this one.

Okay, actually, even if you have a lot of money, these needs may not be satisfied.

Oh, really?

Yes, because to satisfy these needs, they need something else other than money.

So, money alone cannot satisfy these needs.

On the other hand, some of these needs may be satisfied with little or no money.

So, we may not need a lot of money?

Yes, this is why people need to be clear on why they want a lot of money.

You mean after the lower level needs are satisfied?

Yes, after the lower level needs are satisfied, why do they want a lot of money?

Is this why you didn't need a lot of money to live a meaningful life on Earth?

Sure, to live a meaningful life is to do with the higher level needs.

So, we don't need money to make the world go round after all?

Well, in a physical, practical society, you still need money for your basic living.

Chapter 2

Conversation with Guru Harry (Part 2)

Guru Harry, since we need money to live physically on Earth, I have a question I like to ask you about money.

Ask, and it shall be answered.

How should we manage our money?

Okay, let's manage our money.

Now let's assume that I have just graduated from a university and started working.

Congratulations!

Thank you, and I am in this big, wide world.

Sure, let's put life into a perspective first.

What perspective?

How many years do you expect to live?

About eighty.

How many years have you spent in studying?

About twenty.

So, how many years do you have left in your present incarnation?

About sixty.

How many years do you expect to be working?

About forty.

Very good, Tom. So this is your starting point.

What is the point?

Have a financial plan such that your earnings from forty years are sufficient to cover your expenses for sixty years.

You mean I should save while I earn so that I can use the savings to cover my retirement expenses.

Well, this is the starting point.

What is the next point?

There is another reason why you should save.

What is the other reason?

Retrenchment.

You mean being out of work?

Yes, there is a high chance for you to be out of work during your working life.

Well, if I'm out of work, it's not exactly a working life.

So, you also need savings to cover your expenses while you are out of work.

Whoa, so I better start saving!

Yep, once you start earning, the first thing you should to do is to save.

Wow, we are really going into the money world!

And you know there is a saying?

What is the saying?

Earnings more than expenses equal happiness. Earnings less than expenses equal misery.

Is this why so many people live in misery?

Yes, too many.

So, we really should manage our earnings prudently?

Yes, you should.

But how?

Okay, divide your earnings into three portions.

What is the first portion?

The first portion is for your present expenses.

What is the second portion?

The second portion is for your future expenses.

What are future expenses?

Your out of work and retirement expenses.

What is the third portion?

The third portion is for buying your house.

Hold on. Why is this a separate item?

Because a house is usually the single most expensive item anyone buys during his lifetime, and the repayment period can last for decades.

I see.

So, if you have bought a house, whatever earnings you receive each month, it should immediately go into the first and third portions.

Will I have anything left?

Whatever is left goes into your second portion.

So, I may not have anything left?

This is called hand to mouth.

Or stop working, stop eating.

Yes, these people will find it difficult to retire.

They cannot retire.

Suppose your earnings are more than the first and third portions, then you can have savings in your second portion.

Then, I can retire.

Out of this second portion, you need to invest it wisely.

How?

Divide it into four sub-portions.

What is the first sub-portion?

The first sub-portion is to leave an amount in your savings account, which may be called the emergency money.

What is emergency money?

This is money for you to use in case of any emergency, such as losing your job.

But the interest rate in savings account is very low.

Well, it is better to keep your money there because otherwise you may have to borrow money during an emergency, which is usually charged at very high interest rate.

So, I save on the borrowing.

And it's a great saving.

What is the second sub-portion?

The second sub-portion may be called the cash component which is putting an amount into fixed deposits.

Because the fixed deposit interest rates are usually higher than those in savings account.

Yes, but it is also less liquid.

And since the interest rate for the longer term fixed deposit is usually higher than the shorter term fixed deposit, it is better to put money into the longer term fixed deposit, right?

Hmm, not necessarily.

How come?

Because the trend is more important than the absolute interest rates.

Can you elaborate?

Let's say the interest rate is on a rising trend.

Okay, the interest rate is rising.

Then, it is better to put the money into short term fixed deposit.

Why?

Because when the fixed deposit matures and gets rolled over, it can then enjoy a higher interest rate.

What happens if the interest rate is on a falling trend?

It is then better to put the money into a long term fixed deposit.

Why?

So that it can enjoy the higher interest rate for a longer period.

What is the third sub-portion?

The third sub-portion may be called the fixed income component which is putting an amount into bonds or preferential shares.

What are bonds and preferential shares?

These are financial instruments that give out a fixed return?

Why do we put money there?

Because the returns from bonds and preferential shares are usually higher than those from fixed deposits.

So, why don't we put all our money into bonds and preferential shares instead of fixed deposits?

Well, because money in bonds and preferential shares is less liquid than fixed deposits.

Is there any difference between bonds and preferential shares?

Sure, the coupon rate for preferential shares is usually higher than that for bonds.

What is the coupon rate?

It is like the interest rate in a fixed deposit, except the payout from bonds and preferential shares are usually at a semi-annual interval prior to maturity.

So, why don't we put all our money into preferential shares instead of bonds?

Because preferential shares carry a higher risk than bonds.

Is there any other difference between bonds and preferential shares?

Sure, bonds have a maturity date while preferential shares may not.

What is the implication of the maturity date?

Since bonds have a maturity date, you can then be sure to get back one hundred percent of your capital upon maturity.

How about preferential shares?

Since they may not have a maturity date, so if you wish to liquidate your shares, you have to sell them at market rate.

Which means I may get more or less than my initial capital.

Indeed, which brings us to the interest rate.

What about the interest rate?

Well, the interest rate affects the bonds and preferential shares prices?

How?

You see the interest rate can go up or down over time, while the coupon rate is fixed.

So?

So, if the interest rate is on an upward trend, the bonds and preferential shares prices will usually come down.

And if the interest rate is on a downward trend, the bonds and preferential shares prices will usually go up.

Very good, Tom.

Which means the best time to buy bonds and preferential shares is when the interest rate is coming down.

Excellent, Tom.

What is the fourth sub-portion?

The fourth sub-portion may be called the equity component which is putting an amount into equities.

Why?

Because the returns from equities can be higher than those from bonds and preferential shares.

So, why don't we put all our money into equities instead of bonds and preferential shares?

Well, because equities have a higher risk than bonds and preferential shares and you may even lose your capital.

So, it's a question of balancing risk with return.

That's right, and you may adjust the amounts in the last three sub-portions according to market condition.

Can you elaborate?

When the equity market is high, you can sell your equities and put your money into the cash or fixed income components.

And when the equity market is low, I can then take the money from the cash or fixed income components and buy more equities.

Again very good, Tom, you are learning fast.

Well, Guru Harry, I am only learning from you.

But then you have to be careful with two misconceptions in investing your money.

Whoa, tell me the misconceptions.

The first one is related to the rate of inflation.

Okay, what about the rate of inflation?

You may be advised not to put your money in a fixed deposit because its return is lower than the rate of inflation.

Hmm, that sounds like a sound advice, right?

Haha, but what happens if the return from a fixed deposit is higher than those of other investments?

Uh, then it is better to put my money in a fixed deposit, right?

Yes Tom, under certain market conditions, it is possible that a fixed deposit gives better return than the other investments.

But it is lower than the rate of inflation.

So what?

But my money is devalued as compared to the rate of inflation.

So what?

Hmm, what do you mean?

I mean if an investment gives you the best return among all the other investments, even though the return is lower than the rate of inflation, it is still better to put your money there, right?

Well yes, so there is no need to compare the return with the rate of inflation?

No Tom, when you are considering where to invest your money, only look at which investment gives you the best return. The rate of inflation is actually irrelevant.

What a revelation! So, comparing an investment return with the rate of inflation is actually a misconception.

Yes, it is also a distraction.

Okay, no more comparing an investment return with the rate of inflation, and no more distraction.

Good, let's move to the second misconception.

Yes, what is the second misconception?

The second misconception is related to risk.

Okay, what about risk?

You know there is a common saying.

What is the saying?

Higher risk, higher return.

Yes, that's a common saying and that's correct, right?

Wrong.

Oh, really.

The saying should actually read "higher risk, higher potential return".

Oh, you mean they've left out the word "potential"?

Yes, and the missing word is critical.

Why?

Because by leaving out that word, the saying actually becomes incorrect and misleading.

You mean it misleads people to think that by putting their money into a high risk investment, their return is higher?

Exactly!

And with the high risk investment, actually only the potential return is higher.

Yes Tom, the actual return could be lower.

In fact, the actual return could be negative.

Haha Tom, by putting your money in a high risk investment, yes it could go down the drain.

I suppose this is why they called the investment high risk.

So, it's not higher risk, higher return.

Nope.

It's higher risk, and the return could be lower.

Or even negative.

So, when you invest, you must be careful with these two misconceptions.

Yes, Guru Harry.

Invest wisely, Tom.

Wisdom for living spiritually with money

Chapter 3

Conversation with Guru Harry (Part 3)

Guru Harry, can we now turn to your spiritual perspective on how money fits into a physical, practical life?

Yes, we can.

So, what is your spiritual perspective on money?

Let's first review what is a spirit, shall we?

Sure, it's a soul, right?

Yes, soul and spirit can be used interchangeably.

The soul or spirit can be considered as the non-physical, spiritual part of us, right?

Very good Tom, so does a soul have any needs?

Nope, souls don't have needs and they live forever.

Well, that's a spiritual belief.

Yes, that's what I choose to believe.

So, if a soul has no needs, does it need money?

Of course not.

There you are, that's the spiritual perspective on money.

Uh, is that it?

Yes, a soul doesn't have any needs. So, it surely doesn't need money, and it lives forever.

I know, but is there more to it than that?

Nope, that's the complete spiritual perspective on money.

Guru Harry, you are having me on.

Haha Tom, yes I'm pulling your leg.

Whew, that's a relief.

Okay, let's really explore the spiritual perspective on money, shall we?

Sure, let's explore.

You see if a soul lives on its own, it doesn't have any needs.

No needs.

So, it doesn't need money.

Nope, it doesn't need a single cent.

But what happens when a soul lives with a body?

You mean when a soul lives in a body?

Yeah, when a soul and a body are living together as a human with a soul, do they have any needs?

Hmm, this is a tricky one.

Does the soul have any needs when it lives with a body?

I know what you are asking, Guru Harry, but I really don't know the answer.

Okay, since a soul can survive without any needs, then it can still survive without any needs even though it is with a body, right?

Yes, a soul has no needs with and without a body.

But does the body have any needs?

Sure, the body has many needs, as summarized in the Maslow's hierarchy of needs.

So, when a soul and a body are living together, do they have any needs?

This is what you asked me earlier?

Yes, what is your answer now?

Okay, let me try to answer the question this time.

Good, give it a try.

Well, since a soul doesn't have needs, and a body has many needs, when they live together, I suppose they may have some needs.

Good try, Tom! Yes, this is a tricky one.

Yes, Guru Harry, at least it is tricky for me.

Okay, let me clarify.

Please do.

When a soul is living with a body, and if it wants the body to survive, then the combined soul and body has needs.

Ah, that's the answer and it makes sense.

And the needs are the same as the body living on its own.

You mean a body without a soul?

Yes, a physical body only.

And the needs are the survival needs of a body?

If the body wants to survive.

Okay, so the needs of a body living on its own are the same as those of a combined soul and body?

The needs are the same but the ways to satisfy them are different.

What is the difference?

For a body living without a soul, the body decides on how to satisfy the needs purely on the physical level.

What happens when the body is living with a soul?

The soul guides the body on how to satisfy the needs.

You mean the soul adds a spiritual dimension?

Yes, this is the role of the soul.

You mean bringing the spiritual dimension to the body?

Yes, and when it comes to money, the soul looks at it from a spiritual perspective.

I see. So, what is the spiritual perspective on money?

Well, let's use a riddle to look at money, shall we?

Sure, I love riddles.

Let's suppose there is a ten-dollar note on the table, will you take it?

Hmm, is it ok for me to take it?

Yes, it's ok.

Is it legal for me to take it?

Yes, it's perfectly legal.

Will anybody know if I take the money?

Nope, nobody will know unless you tell them.

Is there a catch?

Nope, no catch.

Are there any strings attached?

No, no strings attached.

Are there any consequences after I take the money?

The only consequence is that you will be ten dollars richer.

Can I spend the money?

Sure, after you've taken the money, you can spend it whichever way you like.

So, it's legal, no catch, no strings attached and no bad consequences if I take the money?

That's right.

Sounds like it's ok for me to take the money?

That's what I told you earlier.

But I'm still hesitant, Guru Harry.

The ten-dollar note is there for the taking.

What happens to the ten-dollar note if I don't take it?

Somebody else may take it.

Oh, in that case, I'll take the ten-dollar note.

Congratulations!

Thank you.

You are ten dollars richer.

Wow, I never thought money can come so easily.

Now, let's suppose there is a one-hundred-dollar note on the table, will you take it?

Hmm, is it ok for me to take it?

Yes, it's ok.

Is it legal for me to take it?

Yes, it's perfectly legal.

Will anybody know if I take the money?

Nope, nobody will know unless you tell them.

Is there a catch?

Nope, no catch.

Are there any strings attached?

No, no strings attached.

Are there any consequences after I take the money?

The only consequence is that you will be one hundred dollars richer.

Can I spend the money?

Sure, after you've taken the money, you can spend it whichever way you like.

So, it's legal, no catch, no strings attached and no bad consequences if I take the money?

That's right.

Sounds like it's ok for me to take the money?

That's what I told you earlier.

But I'm still hesitant, Guru Harry.

The one-hundred-dollar note is there for the taking.

What happens to the one-hundred-dollar note if I don't take it?

Somebody else may take it.

Oh, in that case, I'll take the one-hundred-dollar note.

Congratulations!

Thank you.

You are one hundred dollars richer.

Wow, I never thought money can come so easily.

Now, let's suppose there is a one-thousand-dollar note on the table, will you take it?

Whoa, Guru Harry, this is getting too much.

You mean one thousand dollars is too much?

I mean there is more and more money on the table.

Well, that's the riddle.

Yeah, I know but I don't feel comfortable taking one thousand dollars.

You mean you are comfortable taking ten dollars and one hundred dollars, but not one thousand dollars?

Well, taking a small sum of money may be alright. I'm worried that something bad might happen if I take the one-thousand-dollar note.

Let me assure you that nothing bad will happen.

So, it is ok for me to take the money?

Yes, it's ok.

Is it legal for me to take it?

Yes, it's perfectly legal.

Will anybody know if I take the money?

Nope, nobody will know unless you tell them.

Is there a catch?

Nope, no catch.

Are there any strings attached?

No, no strings attached.

Are there any consequences after I take the money?

The only consequence is that you will be one thousand dollars richer.

Can I spend the money?

Sure, after you've taken the money, you can spend it whichever way you like.

So, it's legal, no catch, no strings attached and no bad consequences if I take the money?

That's right.

Sounds like it's ok for me to take the money?

That's what I told you earlier.

But I'm still hesitant, Guru Harry.

The one-thousand-dollar note is there for the taking.

What happens to the one-thousand-dollar note if I don't take it?

Somebody else may take it.

Oh, in that case, I'll take the one-thousand-dollar note.

Congratulations!

Thank you.

You are one thousand dollars richer.

Wow, I never thought money can come so easily.

Now, let's suppose there is a ten-thousand-dollar note on the table, will you take it?

Guru Harry, this is getting ridiculous.

No, there is a ten-thousand-dollar note on the table, and you can take it if you want.

This is making me nervous.

You mean you are okay taking a ten-dollar note, a one-hundred-dollar note and even a one-thousand-dollar note, but when it comes to taking a ten-thousand-dollar note, you are feeling nervous?

Yeah, because the amount is getting big.

Let me assure you that there is nothing to be nervous about and the ten-thousand-dollar note is there for the taking.

So, it is ok for me to take the money?

Yes, it's ok.

Is it legal for me to take it?

Yes, it's perfectly legal.

Conversation with Guru Harry

Will anybody know if I take the money?

Nope, nobody will know unless you tell them.

Is there a catch?

Nope, no catch.

Are there any strings attached?

No, no strings attached.

Are there any consequences after I take the money?

The only consequence is that you will be ten thousand dollars richer.

Can I spend the money?

Sure, after you've taken the money, you can spend it whichever way you like.

So, it's legal, no catch, no strings attached and no bad consequences if I take the money?

That's right.

Sounds like it's ok for me to take the money?

That's what I told you earlier.

But I'm still hesitant, Guru Harry.

The ten-thousand-dollar note is there for the taking.

What happens to the ten-thousand-dollar note if I don't take it?

Somebody else may take it.

Oh, in that case, I'll take the ten-thousand-dollar note.

Congratulations!

Thank you.

You are ten thousand dollars richer.

Wow, I never thought money can come so easily.

Now, let's suppose there is a one-hundred-thousand-dollar note on the table, will you take it?

Guru Harry, this is getting scary.

You mean you are okay taking a ten-dollar note to a ten-thousand-dollar note, but when it comes to taking a one-hundred-thousand-dollar note, you are finding it scary?

Yeah, because the amount is bigger than big.

Exactly, imagine how many things you can do with one hundred thousand dollars.

So, it is ok for me to take the money?

Yes, it's ok.

Is it legal for me to take it?

Yes, it's perfectly legal.

Will anybody know if I take the money?

Nope, nobody will know unless you tell them.

Is there a catch?

Nope, no catch.

Are there any strings attached?

No, no strings attached.

Are there any consequences after I take the money?

The only consequence is that you will be one hundred thousand dollars richer.

Can I spend the money?

Sure, after you've taken the money, you can spend it whichever way you like.

So, it's legal, no catch, no strings attached and no bad consequences if I take the money?

That's right.

Sounds like it's ok for me to take the money?

That's what I told you earlier.

But I'm still hesitant, Guru Harry.

The one-hundred-thousand-dollar note is there for the taking.

What happens to the one-hundred-thousand-dollar note if I don't take it?

Somebody else may take it.

Oh, in that case, I'll take the one-hundred-thousand dollar note.

Congratulations!

Thank you.

You are one hundred thousand dollars richer.

Wow, I never thought money can come so easily.

Now, let's suppose there is a one-million-dollar note on the table, will you take it?

Guru Harry, I don't want to play this game anymore.

Oh, what's wrong, Tom?

Because it is getting beyond ridiculous. I mean who would leave a one-million-dollar note on the table?

Okay, let's take it as a game, and imagine hypothetically there is a one-million-dollar note on the table, will you take it?

It's a lot of money to take.

Exactly, imagine how much good you can do with one million dollars.

So, it is ok for me to take the money?

Yes, it's ok.

Is it legal for me to take it?

Yes, it's perfectly legal.

Will anybody know if I take the money?

Nope, nobody will know unless you tell them.

Is there a catch?

Nope, no catch.

Are there any strings attached?

No, no strings attached.

Are there any consequences after I take the money?

The only consequence is that you will be one million dollars richer.

Can I spend the money?

Sure, after you've taken the money, you can spend it whichever way you like.

So, it's legal, no catch, no strings attached and no bad consequences if I take the money?

That's right.

Sounds like it's ok for me to take the money?

That's what I told you earlier.

But I'm still hesitant, Guru Harry.

The one-million-dollar note is there for the taking.

What happens to the one-million-dollar note if I don't take it?

Somebody else may take it.

Oh, in that case, I'll take the one-million-dollar note.

Congratulations!

Thank you.

You are one million dollars richer.

Wow, I never thought money can come so easily.

Now, let's suppose there is a ten-million-dollar note on the table, will you take it?

Guru Harry, this is only a game, right?

Yes, it's only a game.

Okay, I'll take the money.

Oh, I see, now let's suppose it is not just a game, it is for real.

You mean there is really a ten-million-dollar note on the table?

Yes, will you take it?

If it is for real, then I have to think about it.

Okay, you know ten million dollars will make you financially free.

You mean I don't have to work for another day of my life?

Nope, you can simply relax and enjoy life.

You mean I can start my retirement?

Sure, and do you know how many would love to retire early?

You mean I can retire early?

Only if you take the ten million dollars.

Okay, I'll take the ten-million-dollar note.

Congratulations!

Thank you.

You are ten million dollars richer, and you are financially free.

Hooray, I can start my retirement right here right now!

So, in all the instances in the riddle, you have taken the money.

Yes, because you said it's okay to take them.

Haha Tom, since you have taken the money, you also have to take the responsibility.

You mean I am responsible for my actions?

Yes, and it doesn't matter who advised you to take the money.

You mean that includes you?

Actually, it also includes God.

Wow really, but many people follow the word of God.

Yes, it's called religion.

But they are still responsible for their own actions.

Well, God isn't going to take the responsibility for them.

I see.

Anyway, let's take a look at what the masters would have done in the riddle.

Yes definitely, I must take a look at this.

Okay, here comes the masters...

Chapter 4

Conversation with Guru Harry (Part 4)

Yes, Guru Harry, how would the masters respond to the riddle?

Okay Tom, this is what I'm going to share with you now.

Great, cause I really want to know whether the masters would have taken the money.

The masters would not have taken the money.

You mean any of it?

The masters would not take what is not theirs.

You mean the money on the table is not theirs?

So, they wouldn't take it.

But I've taken it.

The masters would not take any money if they haven't earned it.

You mean they have not earned the money on the table?

So, they wouldn't take it.

But I've taken it.

The masters would not take any money that they don't deserve having it.

You mean they have not done anything to deserve having the money on the table?

So, they wouldn't take it.

But I've taken it.

You know there is a saying, Tom?

What is the saying?

Masters know that it's not the ability to make money that counts. It's the ability to say "no" to money that counts.

Whoa, this is so contrary to what is taught in my society.

Yes, it is, isn't it?

Sure, my society teaches us to grab money whenever and in whatever way we can.

Is your society spiritual?

Hmm, I suppose not.

No Tom, your society cannot be spiritual if they are so crazy about money.

And they are crazy about those who are crazy rich.

And they condemn those who are poor.

That's right, Guru Harry, how do you know?

Because these are the signs of a non-spiritual society.

I see. Can you tell me more about how masters handle money?

Sure, masters know that they don't have to take what is offered to them.

You mean even though what is offered is money?

Yes, masters don't necessarily take even though money is offered to them.

But had the masters taken the ten million dollars, they could retire early.

Masters don't look for retirement.

Then, what do they look for?

They look for ways to serve others.

You mean they look for ways to do good to others?

Yes, masters look forward to their work.

You mean they love their work?

And they work day and night.

You mean they work tirelessly?

But not for money.

Then, what do they work for?

For the betterment of others.

Wow, how noble.

And spiritual.

And practical.

Yes, masters look for practical ways to help others.

Okay, Guru Harry, can we come back to money?

Sure, let's get back to where the money is.

Can you elaborate on how the masters decide whether to take or not to take the money?

Yes, to take or not to take, this is the question.

This is indeed the question, Guru Harry.

And masters are very careful in deciding whether to take or not to take.

You mean money?

They'll want to know where the money comes from.

You mean they want to know the source of the money?

They'll want to know why money is offered to them.

You mean they'll want to know the reason why the money is given to them.

And they'll only take if there is a valid reason.

You mean they'll only take the money if there is a good reason?

Yes, and if the masters take the money, they'll also ensure that they give something of value in return.

You mean like a place in Heaven?

Haha Tom, you are now dabbling into religion.

Well, that's what religion offer, right?

Yes, they take their followers' money and offer them a place in Heaven.

That's not a bad deal, right?

No, actually it's a very good deal.

I mean it's a very good deal for the followers.

Yes, to be able to buy a place in Heaven can't be bad.

But can we really buy a place in Heaven?

No, they don't call it "buy", they call it "donate".

Or "accumulate merit".

Yes, when you donate you accumulate merit, or so they say.

And if you have enough merit, you go to Heaven.

Hallelujah!

Is this why the religious organizations receive so many donations?

You see how rich the religious organizations are.

Whoo, some are super rich.

And they don't have to spend the money to build Heaven.

No, they just created Heaven through thin air.

Because I have to say that it's worth the donation.

Oh, what do you mean?

I mean you only pay money and in return, you get eternal peace and happiness.

Wow, is there such a good deal on Earth?

Well, anything that sounds too good to be true, it probably is.

But the followers will pay?

Yes, unfortunately, many followers will pay and some will pay more than what they can afford.

So that they book a place in Heaven?

I mean who doesn't like to go to Heaven.

But can we really buy a place in Heaven?

Haha Tom, is Heaven for sale?

It seems so according to religion, even though they don't say it in so many words.

But masters don't desire to go to Heaven.

Oh, how come?

Because they can live anywhere as though it is Heaven.

Because Heaven is within?

That's right, Tom. The Kingdom of God is within.

So, they don't accumulate merit?

No Tom. Masters do good only for goodness sake.

But it is still a good deal for the followers.

Actually, it is even a better deal for the religious organizations.

Oh, how is that?

Because they take the money and then offer something to the followers in their afterlife.

You mean they take your money now and offer the followers something in the future?

Which doesn't exist.

Oh yes, you said that there is no Heaven in our earlier conversations.

Yes, it's better to believe there is no Heaven.

So that we only do good for goodness sake.

And not thinking of accumulating merit.

Nor going to Heaven.

Yes Tom, this is in fact the essence of spiritual living.

You mean this is the core of spiritual living which is not religious?

Yes, masters live spiritually and not religiously.

Can we go back to the part where you said when the masters take the money, they'll give something in return?

Sure, we're back.

So, you mean masters don't just take and take?

Nope, masters take and then give, or give and then take.

And they give something of value in return?

Yes, that's why they don't offer others a place in Heaven.

Then, what do the masters give?

They give something of value here and now.

You mean masters give something of practical value?

Yes, because practical living is spiritual living.

And spiritual living is practical living.

That's right, Tom. Spiritual living is not all about the afterlife.

Of course not, spiritual living is about our present life right here right now, right?

Very good Tom, you are really getting into the heart of spiritual living.

And practical living.

Talking about practical living, do you know why masters don't gamble?

Nope, is there some spiritual reason?

Because in gambling, one man's gain is another man's loss.

Or a woman's loss.

Yes, the winner in gambling basically takes the money from the loser.

Well, that's what gambling is all about.

But as the winner takes the money, there is nothing of value given to the loser.

Only the experience of losing.

This is also why the masters do not buy lottery tickets.

You mean one woman's gain is another woman's loss?

Or a man's loss.

You mean as the winner takes the money, there is nothing of value given to the loser?

That's right. This is also why the masters do not do short-term trading of shares.

You mean one woman's gain is another man's loss?

Because the masters practice "we are all one".

Ah ha, this is the spiritual reason, right?

Yes, so the masters practice "I only win if you also win".

You mean the masters look for win-win and not win-lose situations?

That's right, Tom. The masters are also very particular on how they earn their money.

You mean they'll only do the "right" work to make their money?

The masters will only do work that is of value to a society.

You mean they'll only do work of practical value?

And the masters are not attached to their money.

You mean they are non-attached to their money?

Yes, actually money should be the easiest to be non-attached from.

Oh, how come?

Because it can be easily replaced.

Can you elaborate?

Say if you have lost some money today.

Okay, I lost some money today.

Then, you gain some money tomorrow.

Okay, I gain some money tomorrow.

Then, your loss has been replaced by your gain.

You mean no loss no gain?

I mean you are back to the situation before your loss.

But what happens if I didn't gain back the loss?

Then, take it that the money was not meant to be yours in the first place.

Is this how the masters can be at peace even when they lose money?

Yes Tom, masters know that money can leave them any time.

You mean money can come today, and gone tomorrow?

Yes, this is why masters do not attach themselves to money.

Wisdom for living spiritually with money

Chapter 5

Conversation with Guru Harry (Part 5)

Guru Harry, that was quite a journey on money and spiritual living.

Yes Tom, it's better to see money from a spiritual perspective.

Sure, but how come the masters can say "no" to money so easily?

Because they live their lives differently from the ordinary people.

Oh, can you elaborate?

Okay, let's start with a human who is not a master and sees himself as a body only.

You mean he thinks he is only a human body and nothing else?

Yes, and let's call this human a physical being.

Sure, since he can also see the physical side of his being.

What could be his purpose in life?

I suppose if he thinks he is a body only, his purpose in life could be keeping the body going?

Yes Tom, it's very important to a physical being to keep the body alive.

Why?

Because if he sees himself as the body only, when the body dies, it is the end of him.

Or her.

Yes, the end of both him and her. This is why you see many men and women in your society are scrambling for money.

Yes, I see that alright.

Because money can be used to satisfy the first level of the Maslow's hierarchy of needs.

You mean the basic survival needs?

Yes, and they can live if they have money.

You mean money can be used to satisfy the basic survival needs?

And if they don't have money, they die.

You mean if the basic survival needs are not satisfied, they die?

Yes, so for these people you see, it's a matter of life and death.

Whoa, is it that serious?

For people who are living on the first level needs, it is that serious.

Is this why people are obsessed with making a living?

Sure, they have to make money day and night.

Why?

Because they are living from hand to mouth.

Is this why they also stay in jobs that they don't like?

Sure, some of them stay in jobs that they really hate.

For the whole of their lives?

Yes Tom, some people spend their whole working lives doing things that they don't like.

Because they need the money?

It's deeper than that.

Oh, what is the deeper reason?

Because they see themselves as bodies only.

You mean if the bodies die, they think it's the end of them?

Yes Tom, for those who see themselves as bodies only, living is very important.

Because they don't want to die?

Because they don't want to see themselves extinct.

Because they think when the bodies die, it's the end of them?

Yes, and that's why they are completely focused on the physical survival of their bodies.

And nothing else.

This is also why they are completely focused on making money.

You mean they are committed to live at all costs?

Yes, their purpose in life is to be alive at all costs.

But eventually, they'll still die.

Yes, the truth is that whatever is born is destined to die.

No matter how much time they spend on making money.

No matter how much money they make.

And no matter how much money they have.

Yes Tom, this is the irony in these people's lives. They can spend their whole lives making money, and yet in the end, they die.

Is this why they see longevity as a blessing?

Yes, and they also see it as an achievement.

You mean the longer the better?

That's how they see it.

And more money the better?

Well, I suppose if you want to live longer, you need more money.

So, money is very important to these people?

Yes, I suppose if your purpose is to keep the body alive and you are living on the first level of needs, money is very important.

But after the first level of needs is satisfied, does money become less important?

Yes, it does, but to some people, money is still very important.

Such as?

For those who want to live a lavish lifestyle.

How come?

Because a lavish lifestyle needs a lot of money to maintain, so they want lots and lots of money.

So, money is important to these people too.

Money is also important to those whose status is tied to their wealth.

You mean their status is tied to how much money they have?

And if the money is gone, their status is also gone.

So, money is also important to these people?

Yes, this is why you see so many people in your society are spending their whole lives chasing money.

Even though some of them may already have enough money to live.

Because they are after more than the basic living.

You mean they are after lavish living and high status?

Yes Tom, and these desires need more money than that for basic living.

You mean a lot more money?

That's why you see these people chasing money day and night.

You mean just like those who are struggling for a basic living?

This is why you see both the rich and the poor are chasing money in your society.

Yes, I can see that.

Okay Tom, how about I try a riddle on you now?

Oh, another riddle.

For those who are spending their whole lives in making money, are they masters of money?

Well, if they are spending their whole lives making money, surely they must be the masters of money.

Or are they slaves?

You mean they are slaves to money?

Yes, if they spend their whole lives making money, are they masters or slaves to money?

Haha, good one, Guru Harry, you mean even though they may be good in making money, but they have been enslaved by money?

Yes Tom, you see while the poor may be slaves to money due to their basic survival needs, the rich can also be slaves to money.

You mean due to their undesirable desires?

Yes, so money can enslave both the poor and the rich.

That's happening in my society, right?

Yes, there are too many slaves in your society.

Oh dear, can we now turn to the masters?

Sure, let's see how the masters live differently.

Great, this is what I want to see.

Okay, let's start with the basic difference between a master and an ordinary human.

Oh yes, what is the basic difference between a master and an ordinary human?

A master realizes he is a soul, while an ordinary human thinks he is a body.

You mean the master knows he is not the body?

No Tom, the master knows that he is a spiritual being, while an ordinary human thinks he is a physical being.

Wow, that's a huge difference, right?

Yes, that's an enormous difference because the master knows that when a body dies, he doesn't die.

Because he is not the body.

Very good, Tom, so the purpose of life for a master can't be keeping the body alive.

You mean the master knows that he is a soul and he lives forever?

Yes, forever and a day.

You mean till eternity?

Yes, and the soul can live without any needs.

You mean the master can live without any money?

Sure, since the master has no needs, he doesn't need any money.

So, the master lives "happily" as a soul without any money?

Yes Tom, so if the master doesn't have any needs, what could be his purpose in life?

You mean in his physical life?

Yes, if a master's soul incarnates into a physical human body, what could be the purpose?

Wow, Guru Harry, this is getting deep.

Yes Tom, we are getting to the deep purpose of a soul.

You mean a soul which has incarnated into a body has a purpose?

Yes, what could be the purpose for a soul to live with a body?

Hmm, I afraid this is too deep for me.

Okay, let's take a master who has incarnated into a body and comes to Earth, what could be his purpose?

You mean he may want to do certain work on Earth?

Bingo, Tom, if a master wants to do certain physical work on Earth, then he needs to incarnate in a physical, human body.

So that he can use the body to carry out the physical work on Earth.

Very good Tom, the master comes to Earth in a physical body with a mission.

You mean the master has a mission to accomplish on Earth?

And this mission is his purpose in his physical life with the body.

I see. So, the master lives with a purpose when he is with the body.

To illustrate this point, let me share with you a letter from a grandfather to a grandson.

Sure, I like to read the letter.

It is in Appendix A.

Wow, so life is not about making a living, but living with a higher purpose.

Yes Tom, when you realize you are a soul, you live with a higher purpose.

And that is real spiritual living, right?

Actually, that is also real physical living.

You mean living with a physical body?

Yes, when we use our physical bodies to carry out a mission, it is real physical living.

And it is much better than the mundane physical living like making a living, right?

Sure, in fact this is how humans should live with their bodies.

Why?

Because it is more meaningful.

You mean this is the reason why we are living with our bodies?

Yes Tom, we are souls and have come to Earth to carry out a mission.

You mean we are all missionaries?

But many don't know it.

Because they don't know they are souls and not bodies.

Yes, but the masters know they are missionaries.

Sure, otherwise they wouldn't be masters, right?

And when the missions are completed, the masters leave their bodies.

So sad!

Actually, the masters don't feel sad when they leave their bodies.

Oh, how come?

Because they know that is the purpose of having bodies.

You mean they use the bodies to carry out the mission?

Yes, so when the mission is accomplished, it is time to go.

You mean it is time to leave the bodies?

Yes, and the bodies die.

So, the masters do not consider longevity a blessing?

Nope, not at all, in fact the masters leave the bodies as soon as the work is done.

You mean they don't linger in the bodies unnecessarily?

No, they don't stay in the bodies when there is no more purpose to do so.

And they don't spend their whole lives making money?

Not at all because this is not the purpose for the masters to live in bodies.

You mean their purpose is to use the bodies to do the work on Earth?

That's right, and they also realize that the life of a body is finite.

So?

So, they use as much as the body's life to do the work rather than use it to make money.

So, they don't chase money day and night?

No, in fact they minimize their time on making money so that they have more time to do the work.

You mean the missionary work?

I mean the meaningful work.

You mean the work that is in line with their purpose in life?

Yes, and their true purpose in their physical lives is to carry out their mission.

And not making money.

Very good Tom, you've got it.

But how do they minimize their time on making money?

By living simply.

You mean masters don't live lavishly?

Nope, they live a simple life.

And they don't use money to boost their status.

Nope, their status is not tied to money.

So, their need for money is minimized.

Yes, and this is why money is not so important to the masters.

And this is why the masters can say "no" to money so easily.

Yes Tom, and this is how they can minimize their time on making money.

And maximize their time on doing their work.

Yes, because this is their real purpose in life.

You mean in their physical life?

Yes, when they are living in their physical bodies on Earth.

Wisdom for living spiritually with money

Chapter 6

Conversation with Guru Harry (Part 6)

Guru Harry, are there other aspects of money you would like to share with me?

Yes, there are three more points on money.

Oh good, what is the first?

The first point is on kindness.

Oh, what has kindness got to do with money?

We'll see.

Okay, let's see.

Can you be kind if you are not rich?

How can we be kind when we are not rich?

Oh, why not?

Because we don't have money to give.

Then, just say a few kind words.

You mean kind words are free?

They can be worth more than gold.

How about written words?

That too, if they are kind.

Are there other ways to show our kindness?

Just give a smile.

You mean just give a simple smile?

Or an approving look.

You mean show them that we approve what they do?

Or a sympathetic look.

Oh, of course, be sympathetic to their situation.

And you can do all these without costing a cent.

Wow, Guru Harry, we can give kindness for free.

Yes Tom, you don't have to be rich to be kind.

Super, Guru Harry, are there other points on money?

Let me share with you two points on morality.

You mean morality and money?

Yes, let me start with the first by asking you a question.

Okay, what is the question?

Wealth, health and morality, which is most important?

From the perspective of the rich and powerful, they'll say wealth.

Can you bring wealth with you after the body is gone?

No.

Can you bring health with you after the body is gone?

No.

Can you bring morality with you after the body is gone?

Hmm, this one, I'm not sure. Maybe, maybe not.

Okay, will morality be left somewhere after the body is gone?

You mean it could be attached to the name after the body is gone?

Very good, Tom. With good morality, you can leave a good name.

Forever and a day!

There's a saying you know.

What is the saying?

If you lose your wealth, you lose nothing. If you lose your health, you lose something. If you lose your morality, you lose everything.

You mean this is the relative importance of wealth, health and morality?

Yes, so which is most important?

Morality, of course.

And how does morality compare with wealth?

As compared to losing morality, losing wealth is so unimportant that it is like losing nothing.

Yes Tom, never trade your morality for wealth.

Yes, Guru Harry.

Now, let's continue with the second point by comparing the characteristics of money with those of morality.

Oh good, let's find out the characteristics of money and morality?

Let's start with a saying, shall we?

Sure, what is the saying?

Money comes and goes; morality comes and grows.

So, we should grow our morality rather than our money.

Yet your society grows money rather than morality.

So, my society is rich in money but poor in morality.

Actually, it would have been better if your society is rich in morality and poor in money.

How much better?

You see there's a problem with money.

What is the problem?

You could lose it overnight.

How can that be?

Disaster can hit anybody any time.

You mean disaster can happen to a society any time?

And it can be a man-made or natural disaster.

And both are just as disastrous.

And the money is gone.

You mean the money can be gone like a smoke in a fire?

But nobody can take away your morality.

Oh yes, I can keep my good name even after my body is gone.

Yes Tom, you can have your good name in your physical life and in your afterlife.

So, it's better to have morality than money.

So, it's better to be poor and moral than rich and immoral.

How can that be?

You see if you are rich and immoral, how long can you enjoy life?

You mean only for a limited period and things may catch up with you?

But if you are moral, how long can you keep the good name?

Forever and a day!

Exactly Tom, this is why it's better to choose morality over money.

That's what the masters do, right?

Yes, that's what the masters do.

Okay, Guru Harry, thank you for all your pointers on looking at money from a spiritual perspective.

Sure, it's better to live with money spiritually.

You mean even in a physical, practical society?

Especially in a physical, practical society.

Yes, Guru Harry.

May you live spiritually with money!

Sure, I'll live with money from a spiritual perspective from now on.

Goodbye, Tom!

Goodbye, Guru Harry!

Appendix A

Letter from grandfather to grandson

Dear Grandson

How are you doing?

While you are busy rushing here and there making a living, have you ever thought about the spiritual side of your life? What if there is a soul inside your body? What if you are the soul and not the body? What if your soul has taken the trouble to come all the way to incarnate into your body, and wants to do something on Earth? If this is so, is your life just about making a living so as to feed your body? Do you know that no matter how much you feed your body, eventually it will still die? So, is this what life is all about or is there a higher purpose? Is there a purpose for your soul to incarnate into your body? Maybe this is a good time to think about the purpose of your life. Maybe this is a good time to find out your higher purpose so that your soul together with your body can accomplish the soul purpose before it leaves your body.

May you live a purposeful and meaningful life!

Your Grandfather

(**Extract from** "*Wisdom for Living Spiritually in the Physical*")

About the author

As the author of the "*Spiritual Living*" book series, and the autobiography "*How an Engineering Professor Becomes a Spiritual Philosopher*", Dr. Tommy Wong lives spiritually in the midst of modern Singapore. Nowadays, he serves the world as a freelance consultant and trainer. He is also an editor and has authored five book series and more than 20 books of four different genres: engineering, philosophy, self-help and spirituality.

Since 2009, his books have been available on Amazon and many other online bookstores worldwide. Between 2012-2017, he was featured three times on the Radio 938LIVE programme "*A Slice of Life Hour*". He has also given more than 40 talks at the Singapore Writers Festival, Read Fest, Human Library Singapore, Heartlands Book Club, Booktique bookstore, Financial Services Consumer Association, as well as various Meetup groups. Further information about Dr. Wong's work can be found on the FB page (https://www.facebook.com/wisdomlivelife).

Selected books by Tommy S. W. Wong

Spiritual Living Series

Wisdom for Spiritual Living (2012)

Wisdom for Living as Spiritual Beings (2015)

Wisdom for Living as Spiritual Masters (2016)

Wisdom for Living Spiritually in the Physical (2019)

Wisdom for Living with New Spirituality (2020)

Wisdom on How to Live Life Series

Wisdom on How to Live Life (2010)

Wisdom on How to Live Life - Book 2 (2010)

Wisdom on How to Live Life - Book 3 (2010)

Wisdom on How to Live Life - Book 4 (2011)

Wisdom on How to Live Life - Book 5 (2012)

"Wisdom on How to Live Life" Quotations (2017)

Overcoming Traumas Series

Wisdom for End-of-Life Living (2013)

Wisdom for Living After Being Fired (2014)

Wisdom for Overcoming Disappointment and Depression (2018)

Wisdom for Living in a Coronavirus Pandemic (2020)

Masters of Life Series

Masters of Life on Meaningful Living (2013)

Masters of Life on Good Life and Good Society (2014)

Masters of Life on Transforming Earth into Heaven (2018)

How Sai Baba Attracts Series

How Sai Baba Attracts Without Direct Contact (2009)

How Sai Baba Attracts Without Direct Contact - Book 2 (2011)

Other books

Minimum Wage for Low Wage Workers (2012)

How an Engineering Professor Becomes a Spiritual Philosopher (2016)

Wisdom for Living Happily Ever After (2019)

Wisdom on What is Good and What is Bad (2021)

Wisdom on Life and Death (2022)